TUMSHIE

Dedicated to my Dad, who carved my turnip
when my arms were too tired; and to my Mum
who filled the napkins with excitement.

First published 2020 by Waverley Books, an imprint of
The Gresham Publishing Company Ltd,
31, Six Harmony Row, Glasgow, G51 3BA, Scotland, UK

www.waverley-books.co.uk

ISBN 978-1-84934-532-3

Printed and bound in the EU

I'd like to thank Ron Grosset and Liz Small of Waverley Books, for their
encouragement, indulgence and for letting my first book see the light of
day; my colleague Eleanor Abraham for her ideas, support and general
couthiness; and my family — for inspiring ideas during walks to school,
and watching patiently while this tumshie took root and grew.

TUMSHIE

The Forgotten Halloween Turnip Lantern

Mark Mechan

WAVERLEY BOOKS

I found my pumpkin Dad ... *oof!*

And I've found my tumshie, Elliot.

Dad, what's a tumshie?

Well, it's just a good Scottish name for a turnip. Some folk call it a neep!

Aw, so it's just a wee turnip.

When I was little, everyone carved a Halloween lantern out of their tumshie.

And we took our lanterns with us when we went guising — that's what trick-or-treating was called, because you're in disguise, see?

Let's get these lanterns carved Elliot!

But a tumshie is rock hard, Dad!
Pumpkins are much easier.
And they're bigger and ... orangey-er.

I know Elliot ... but I like a turnip because
it's traditional. It's small and tough.
Carving it into a lantern takes strength!
Willpower ... and several knives and spoons.

Sometimes even dynamite.

Try a taste of neep, Elliot.

Mmmph. Sweet ... and peppery ...
and crunchy.

Urk.
No thanks.

Finished!
My pumpkin is big and
smiley this year, Dad.

My tumshie is too. Except
it's wee and smiley.

Let's put the candles in
and light them up!

Then you turn off the lights — WOW!

And when the candle flame singes the tumshie — aaah!
The beautiful smell of burnt turnip. It reminds me of Halloween when I was younger.

There is no smell quite like it ...

I can think of a smell it's exactly quite like. *Pooh*.

Dad, how did you carry a tumshie *and* your bag of sweeties when you went out guising?

We didn't really have a bag of sweeties, Elliot. We were usually given an apple and nuts, and sometimes money.

In the old days, the tumshie lanterns were supposed to ward off evil spirits, because Halloween was the night before All Saints' Day.

The guisers would go around the neighbourhood playing tricks on folk — like taking people's gates off their hinges!

And of course we played games — like eating treacle scones that were hung on a string from the ceiling — no hands allowed!

And dookin' for apples.

No hands allowed here either.

Well Dad, when we go out trick-or-treating — erm, I mean, guising — we get to see inside all the neighbours' houses. Then we have to tell a joke, and even if it's not funny they still give you loads of sweets and crisps.

It's *amazing!*

Last year I went as a robot. And there was a girl that had a dagger *right through her head* (but it was only a trick one), and there were three princesses all dressed the same.

And you came home carrying your own weight in sweets, Elliot.

Which YOU ate half of, remember?

Did you *really* not have sweets in the olden days Dad?

Of course we did! It wasn't *that* long ago. When I was your age we didn't get quite as much as you do nowadays, though.

Your Granny used to tie up a cloth napkin for your Auntie and me, full of delicious goodies — chocolate drops, monkey nuts and a juicy mandarin.

It seemed SO exciting!

Aw, I love monkey nuts Dad!

Me too. But my favourite
are cola bottles. Or maybe
flying saucers.

Nah, the best ones are the wee
fried eggs. No — the pink shrimps.

Skull crushers!

Toffee apples!

Gummies!

And you couldn't just turn up at the front door and hold open your bag — you had to do a turn.

Like a twirl you mean?

Naw! It means that you sang a wee song, or told some funny jokes —

My jokes are brilliant Dad. Knock! Knock! —

— or even a spooky poem. You could say a few lines from "Tam O' Shanter". Robert Burns wrote that.

But poems are boring!

Not this one; it's more like a scary story.

Tam was riding home one dark and stormy night, when he spotted some glowing lights in the old, ruined church.

Even though he was scared stiff, he climbed off his horse Meg to have a peep.

What did he see, Dad?

There were witches dancing!
And the Devil himself was there — playing the bagpipes!

Suddenly the witches spotted Tam!
They came screeching out after him.

If he'd had his tumshie he could have
scared them off, Dad.

Ha ha! That's true.
Tam scrambled back on
to Meg and galloped for
his life ...

He knew that if he
could cross the bridge,
they couldn't follow.

"Now, do thy speedy utmost, Meg, and win the key-stane o' the brig —

There at them thou thy tail may toss, a running stream they dare na cross."

Did the witches get him, Dad?

Ach, that would be telling!

We'll read it some night and you'll find out Elliot ...

Howdy! Come away in.

There are toffee apples
if you can do a wee turn.

Have you any funny jokes?

Last night was great fun, Dad.
Now it's time to leave the lanterns
out in our back garden.

Will they grow into
more pumpkins and
turnips do you think?

Hmm, I doubt it Elliot.
But they'll keep guard
over our garden
all winter.

It'll soon be Christmas.

Not yet Dad — it'll soon be Bonfire Night!
And that means FIREWORKS!

And my tumshie will still be here to see them.

Let's light them one last time Elliot ...

Watch your fingers Dad!

The speedy gleams the darkness swallow'd;
Loud, deep and lang, the thunder bellow'd:
That night, a child might understand,
The Deil had business on his hand ...

Spooky, Dad!

Just one more page?

See you again next year!

SUPER SKILLS

A Social Skills Group Program for Children with Asperger Syndrome, High-Functioning Autism and Related Disorders

Judith Coucouvanis

Foreword by Brenda Smith Myles

APC

Autism Asperger Publishing Co.
P.O. Box 23173
Shawnee Mission, KS 66283-0173
www.asperger.net

© 2005 by Autism Asperger Publishing Company
P.O. Box 23173
Shawnee Mission, KS 66283-0173
www.asperger.net

**Publisher's Cataloging-in-Publication
(Provided by Quality Books, Inc.)**

Coucouvanis, Judith.
    Super skills : a social skills group program for
children with Asperger syndrome, high-functioning autism
and related challenges / [Judith Coucouvanis].
        p. cm.
        Includes bibliographical references.
        LCCN 2004117212
        ISBN 1-931282-67-6

        1. Autistic children—Rehabilitation. 2. Autistic
children—Education. 3. Social skills in children.
I. Title.

RJ506.A9C68 2005   618.92'8588203
                            QBI04-20052

This book is designed in Blue Moon and Stone Sans

Managing Editor: Kirsten McBride
Editorial Support: Ginny Biddulph

Printed in the United States of America